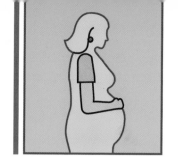

Teens and Pregnancy

A Hot Issue

Ann Byers

Enslow Publishers, Inc.

40 Industrial Road
Box 398
Berkeley Heights, NJ 07922
USA

PO Box 38
Aldershot
Hants GU12 6BP
UK

http://www.enslow.com

Library of Congress Cataloging-in-Publication Data

Byers, Ann.
    Teens and pregnancy: a hot issue / Ann Byers
        p. cm. — (Hot Issues)
    Includes bibliographical references and index.
    Summary: Discusses teen pregnancy as a social problem and outgrowth of the sexual culture in the United States, as well as ways to avoid pregnancy and options for the teen that does become pregnant.
    ISBN 0-7660-1365-0
    1. Teenage pregnancy—United States Juvenile literature. 2. Teenage pregnancy—United States—Prevention Juvenile literature. 3. Teenagers—United States—Sexual behavior Juvenile literature. [1. Teenage mothers. 2. Pregnancy. 3. Women—Health and hygiene. 4. Public welfare.] I. Title. II. Series.
    HQ759.64.B94   2000
    306.874'3—dc21

                          99-37357
                          CIP
                          AC

Printed in the United States of America

10 9 8 7 6 5 4 3 2 1

Illustration Credits: AP/Wide World Photos, pp. 16, 26, 32, 40, 47, 52; © Corel Corporation, pp. 24, 38; © The Stock Market, 1992, p. 11.

Cover Illustration: Background: © Corel Corporation; Foreground: Digital imagery® © 1999 PhotoDisc, Inc.

Contents

Chapter 1

The Problem of Teen Pregnancy

After Michelle's parents divorced, her father had little to do with her. Michelle's mother had problems of her own, including drinking a lot. Neither parent was able to give Michelle much guidance. "I grew up pretty much by myself," Michelle remembers.

Victor was a couple years older than Michelle. When he paid attention to her and told her that he loved her, Michelle believed him. They had sex several times, and when she was seventeen, she had a baby. Victor did not stick around after their baby, Joseph, was born.

Without the baby's father or much help from her parents, Michelle had to care for her baby boy while she finished high school. She transferred to a school that had a nursery on campus. Joseph was cared for in the nursery while Michelle went to class. Going to classes while being a mother was not easy. After she graduated, Michelle went on welfare and moved into her own apartment.

Life after high school was even harder for

Michelle. She got a job in a clothing store, but finding child care was difficult. Her job required her to work some evenings and weekends, and most child-care centers were only open weekdays. When she found a woman who would baby-sit for her, Michelle enrolled in junior college. But when Joseph was sick, she could not take him to the baby-sitter. She frequently missed classes and sometimes could not get to work. She felt frustrated and discouraged. It seemed she spent more time on the bus than she did with her son. The money never seemed to stretch far enough. Michelle was tired all the time and lonely.

So when Victor came back into her life, Michelle let him move in. Before long, she was pregnant again. When she was nineteen, Michael was born and Victor was long gone. He was not in the delivery room when his son came into the world. He was not in the hospital when doctors repaired the hole in his baby's heart. He will not be around to see his children grow up.

Now Michelle is a single mother of two boys. She is still working and attending college. "I'm going to give my children a better life than I had," she says. Michelle is on the bus with her sons by seven in the morning, rain or shine. She drops Joseph off at day care and takes Michael to another sitter. Then she heads for school. In the afternoon, she rides the bus to her job. By the time she picks up her children, Michelle has already put in a twelve-hour day. Then she spends the evening cooking, studying, and caring for her children.

Michelle is luckier than some other young mothers. She has friends she can talk to on the really hard days. She has someone who will baby-sit sometimes when a child is sick and cannot go to day care. But she worries about holding on to her job and keeping up with her class work. She wonders how long it will take her to get off welfare. She hopes she really can give her children a better life.[1]

Michelle's situation is not unusual. One million girls like her get pregnant in the United States every year—almost two every minute. Half of those actually give birth and become teen moms. About one in four has a second pregnancy while still a teen.[2] Their children often have health problems. The fathers are typically older. They are usually legal adults. Very often they leave before the babies are born. Very often the teenagers become single mothers.

How serious is the problem of teen pregnancy? Why are so many young people having babies? What does teen childbearing do to the mothers? The fathers? The children?

Trends

The number of teens who get pregnant each year is an estimated figure. Every pregnancy has three possible outcomes: (a) a live birth; (b) an abortion, which is a deliberate termination of the pregnancy; or (c) a miscarriage or stillbirth, which are unintended terminations of the pregnancy. Some abortions and many miscarriages are not reported to any medical agency, so researchers can only estimate how many occur. The most commonly accepted figures today are these: About 34 percent of teen pregnancies end in abortion and 14 percent in miscarriage, leaving 52 percent resulting in live birth.[3] Therefore, the teen pregnancy rate is roughly double the teen birthrate.

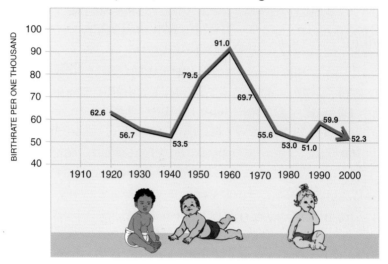

TEEN BIRTHRATES
Births per 1,000 women age 15–19

BIRTHRATE PER ONE THOUSAND

91.0

79.5

69.7

62.6

59.9

56.7

53.5

55.6

53.0 51.0

52.3

100
90
80
70
60
50
40

1910 1920 1930 1940 1950 1960 1970 1980 1990 2000

Sources: Kristin Luker, *Dubious Conceptions: The Politics of Teenage Pregnancy* (Cambridge, Mass.: Harvard University, 1996), p. 196; S.J. Ventura, et. al., "Births: Final Data for 1997." *National Vital Statistics Reports*, vol. 47, no. 18, (Hyattsville, Md.: National Center for Health Statistics, 1999).

The current teen birthrate in the United States (the number of births for every one thousand girls aged fifteen to nineteen) is approximately 58.9.[4] This means that almost 10 percent of all teenage girls have babies. This number is not higher than in previous years. Actually, fewer teens are having babies now than in many earlier decades. The teen birthrate was lower in 1990 than in 1920. It was highest between 1955 and 1960. Although the teen birthrate rose 18 percent from 1985 to 1990, the percentage of adolescents giving birth has been steadily declining since 1991.[5]

The huge difference from four or even two decades ago is that more children are born to unmarried teens than ever before. Forty years ago, adolescents tended to marry before their babies were born, if not before they were conceived. In 1960, fewer than 15 percent of all teen births were to unwed girls.[6] By 1981, 50 percent of teen births occurred outside marriage, and in 1994, 76 percent.[7] So although a smaller proportion of teen girls is getting pregnant and having babies than in the 1960s and 1970s, a much greater percentage is remaining single. Of the half million babies born each year to teen parents, three hundred eighty-four thousand are born to unmarried teenagers.

Problems

The births of so many babies to young, unmarried parents have created a number of problems. One problem is the health risk to the mother and the baby. Young mothers are more likely to have complications during pregnancy and delivery. The younger a woman is, the greater the chance she will be anemic, have high blood pressure, and have a premature or extra-long labor. Unwed teenagers often do not tell their parents they are pregnant until late in the pregnancy, so many do not receive medical care as early as they should. Others, some of whom have no insurance, receive no care before the baby is born. This means they do not have a doctor's help in avoiding the medical problems that sometimes occur in a teen pregnancy.

Babies born to teenage mothers sometimes weigh less than babies born to older mothers. The organs of low-birth-weight babies may not be completely developed. Some are born with problems in their lungs, heart, or brain. Babies who weigh less than 5.5 pounds are forty times more likely to die in their first month of life.[8] Teenage mothers increase the risk of health problems in their children if they do not eat well when they are pregnant and if they drink alcohol, smoke cigarettes, or take drugs.

Teen pregnancy, especially in unmarried teens, can create not only health difficulties, but also economic hardships. Teenage mothers and fathers tend to drop out of school to find jobs so they can support themselves and their babies. With little education, teen parents find themselves locked into low-paying jobs.[9] If the father is out of the picture, the teen mom often must support herself and her child and pay for child care on a very small salary. Little time or money is left to allow the parent to complete her education or qualify for a better job.

Poorly educated parents frequently produce poorly educated children. In fact, children of teenage mothers often do not do as well as other children in a number of areas. Their school performance is lower and their behavior more troublesome. Sometimes the stress on young parents of raising a child with little help or resources can erupt in child abuse or neglect.

These are the realities faced every year by three hundred eighty-four thousand girls in the United States under the age of twenty.

Teen Mothers

Who are these girls? They come from every ethnic group and every socioeconomic category. Still, some girls seem more likely than others to get pregnant and have babies in their teens. Those with the highest rates of teen births are nonwhite adolescents who grow up in poor neighborhoods, live in single-parent homes, and do poorly in school.[10]

Nonwhite. In general, the teen birthrate for

*I*t is important for a teen mother to keep up with her studies and stay in school. Often, pregnant teenagers drop out of school to find jobs so that they can support themselves and their babies.

minorities is about twice as high as for Caucasian youth. The gap between whites and nonwhites narrows only slightly when considering pregnancies rather than births. About 60 percent of African-American and Hispanic teens terminate their pregnancies intentionally.[11] The reason for the higher number of births among minorities is that minority adolescents tend to live in low-income neighborhoods, and more teens in low-income areas become pregnant.

Poverty. The factor most commonly associated with high teen pregnancy rates, the number-one predictor of teen pregnancy, is poverty. In every ethnic group, most of the girls who become teen moms grow up in homes in which the average yearly income is more than nine thousand dollars below the national average.[12] The extra difficulties of raising a child while young, unmarried, and without a high school diploma keep many young mothers in poverty, but most were poor before they became teen moms. Eighty percent of teens who have babies live in or near poverty long before they become pregnant. In their low-income neighborhoods, they have little to do, little to look ahead to, and little reason to delay sexual pleasure.[13]

Single-parent homes. Teenage mothers come from homes with only one parent nearly twice as often as from families with two parents. Usually the single parent is a mother, and she is very likely to have been a teen mom herself. Sometimes the daughters follow the example of their mothers. In general, adolescents in single-parent homes have less money and less parental supervision.[14] Because they have less money, they have less access to birth control. Even when birth control is available at no cost, they may not be able to afford transportation to a free clinic. Because they are often left unsupervised, they have more opportunities to become pregnant.

Poor school performance. Girls who do poorly in school are more likely to bear children early than those who do well.[15] When their grades are low, teens do not feel good about themselves. They turn to activities at which they can succeed (such as having sex) and to people who tell them nice things about themselves (such as people who want to have sex with them). Parents of high achievers are usually very interested in keeping their daughters from becoming pregnant. These parents often encourage their children to avoid situations that might lead to pregnancy. If their warnings fail, parents of high achievers quite frequently pay for abortions for their daughters. However, parents of low achievers, especially poor ones, are sometimes not as upset about the possibility of their children becoming pregnant. They may not have high goals for their girls and may see motherhood as one way their daughters can "make something" of them-selves.[16]

The Fathers

Like adolescent mothers, the fathers of children born to teen moms tend to be poor, fail to achieve in school, and have low goals for themselves. The most significant difference between teen mothers and the fathers of their children is their age. The fathers are almost always older than the girls. Two thirds of the fathers of babies born to teenage mothers are not teenagers.[17] Half of the fathers are five or more years older than the girl, and the younger the girl is, the greater usually is the difference in age.[18] And increasingly, the fathers are not marrying their babies' mothers.

The rise in births to unmarried teens has affected every structure and institution of society: the family, the neighborhood, the school, the workplace, the government, the entertainment industry, the church. At the same time, changes in these institutions have created a context in which teen pregnancy has become common.

Chapter 2

Teens at Risk

Casual sex and pregnancy were "givens" in Esther's world. She had been born when her mother was still in high school, and she had lived with one after another of her mother's boyfriends. Most of the women Esther grew up with—aunts, cousins, friends—had boyfriends and babies when they were young. Esther did not expect anything different for herself.

When she became pregnant at fifteen, Esther knew just how she would handle the situation. "I'm going to go on welfare," she decided, "so I can get an apartment." Esther was simply doing what her mother had done. "My mom will watch the baby so I can finish school," she planned. "I'm too young to have a baby, but it will work out." After all, as far as Esther could see, everything had worked out for her mother.

Today, at twenty-five, Esther and her boyfriend are still together. They work as child-care attendants at the high school center their baby attended, making minimum wage. Three of Esther's four sisters also became teen mothers.[1]

Esther did not intend to get pregnant; she only intended to have sex. But sex can lead to pregnancy, and American teens are more active sexually now than at any other time in history. Before they turn fifteen, more than one third of all adolescents in the United States have had intercourse.[2] By the time they finish high school, over half have begun sexual activity.[3] These figures indicate a sizable increase over those from 1970. Today, more than one half of all teen women admit to having sex before they are married. In 1970, fewer than one third reported having premarital sex.[4]

So although the teen pregnancy rate has actually begun to fall, the rate of adolescent sexual activity remains high. Underlying the steady rise in teen sex are three major factors: (a) the presence of references to sex throughout the environment in which adolescents live, (b) the permissive attitudes of many people in modern society, and (c) the diminishing influence of parents upon their children.

Sexual Culture

The world of the United States teenager is filled with sex. The songs they sing, the magazines they read, the television they watch, the jokes they tell, the games they play—so much is about sex. Sex sells products, sex gets movies good reviews, and sexual experience is a measure of "coolness." Adolescents are surrounded by messages that having sex while still a teenager is normal and expected; not having sex is old-fashioned, babyish, and not "with it."

These messages come across loud and clear in the entertainment media. From late afternoon, when school ends, through the evening viewing hours, sixty-five thousand sexual references are

*C*andice Smith, who became pregnant at age fourteen, hugs her two-year-old daughter, Mariah, in a day-care center in Las Vegas. Nevada has the second-highest teen pregnancy rate in the United States.

made on television every year.[5] Sexual talk or behavior is presented at least once every four minutes on network prime-time programs.[6] In the twenty-two hours of television teens average per week, they see at least fifteen thousand sexual incidents or allusions to sex every year.[7] And the majority of sexual activity and suggestion on TV takes place between people who are not married to each other.[8]

The same type of content that fills the small screen floods the big screen as well. Sixty-seven percent of the movies rated by the Motion Picture Association of America in 1989—more than two thirds—carried an R rating, indicating explicit sex, violence, or profanity.[9] In many theaters, the R rating does not restrict teen viewing, as originally intended, but instead attracts teenagers. Even in movies with lesser ratings, sex between teenage partners is portrayed as exciting, fun, and absolutely commonplace. Seldom in the movies or on TV does premarital sex lead to pregnancy or other serious consequences, such as sexually transmitted diseases.

Music rarely links sex to pregnancy either, and sex-saturated songs fill the waking moments of virtually every adolescent. Teenagers wake up to music, drive to school in cars or buses with it playing, do their homework to its tempo, plug it into their ears as they go to sleep. Everything about the vast majority of modern music—the lyrics, the visual images, the lifestyles of the performers, the activities at concerts—says, "Have a sexual celebration . . .

Ages of Mothers and Fathers of Children Born to Teens

Mothers:		Fathers:	
✓ Under 15	2.3%	✓ Under 16	8%
✓ 15-17	35.4%	✓ 16-17	27%
✓ 18-19	62.3%	✓ 18 and over	65%

Source: Kristin Luker, *Dubious Conceptions: The Politics of Teenage Pregnancy* (Cambridge, Mass.: Harvard University Press, 1996), p. 201.

BIRTHRATES OF
UNMARRIED TEENS AND WOMEN

Rates are per 1,000 females in specified age group

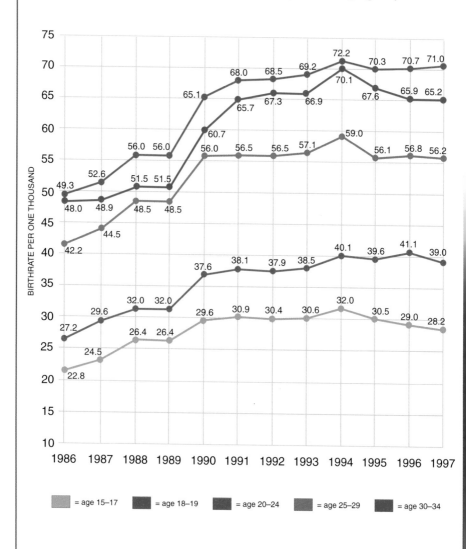

Source: "Table POP6.A Birth Rates for unmarried women by age of mother, 1980-97," *ChildStats.gov*, 1999, <http://www.childstats.gov/ac1999/xpop6a.htm> (January 24, 2000).

feel good . . . feel sexy . . . everyone is doing it."[10] On MTV, which is available in 55 million homes in the United States, 75 percent of the music videos have sexual imagery.[11]

Even if adolescents were to turn off their TVs, radios, and personal stereos, the invitation to indulge their sexuality is still all around them. Teen magazines such as *Sassy* offer instruction on "Sex for Absolute Beginners."[12] Billboards sell items with provocative pictures. Tabloid newspapers report sex scandals in shameless detail. On the Internet, sexual information, fantasy, and pornography are just a click away.

Permissive Society

Thirty-five years ago, such bold expressions of sexual material were not permitted. Television producers allowed no references to sex, even among married couples. Although Lucille Ball was expecting a baby, no one on the *I Love Lucy* show could utter the sensitive word *pregnant*.[13] People treated intercourse as a private matter and considered public mention of sex inappropriate. Sex was not a topic for entertainment or advertising, at least not in adolescent or family settings.

But the "sexual revolution" of the 1960s changed society's attitude toward sexual conduct. Young people rejected the standards and restraints of their parents and other authorities. They sought freedom to express themselves. And society yielded to the "modern" thinking. During the late 1960s and 1970s, the once taboo subject of sex began to pop up everywhere.

➤ The people of the hippie movement praised the virtues of "free love."

➤Antiviolence protests encouraged young people to "make love, not war."

➤*Laugh-In* and other popular TV programs made sex a topic of comedy.

In less than one generation, the societal attitude toward sex had radically changed. Thinking of the past was that sex was an undiscussed secret that properly belongs to husband and wife. The new thought considered sex a natural drive that no one should deny. From there, it was a small step to accepting, even expecting, that adolescents would give full vent to their sexual feelings.

Decreasing Influence of Parents

The people who have, traditionally, taught teenagers to control the expression of their sexual feelings are their parents. But the influence of parents is waning. Teens today spend less time with their mothers and fathers and more with their friends and their entertainment. The parents of most teenagers work outside the home, leaving them little time to spend with their children. Teenagers report that they spend about two hours a week discussing things that are important to them with their mothers and about one hour with their fathers.[14] That is barely three hours a week of parental involvement—if a child lives with two parents—as compared with the average of twenty-two hours in front of the television set.

The growing number of homes with single parents and two-worker parents has left many teenagers with two or more hours to themselves every day. This unsupervised time might be an opportunity to engage in sexual activity. More than half of all teens say they had their first sexual intercourse in their or their partner's home. One study found that 78 percent of sexually active teens used their own bedrooms for sex.[15]

Providing opportunity is not the only way the lack of parental involvement encourages teen sexual activity. Teenagers, like all people, need love and expressions of affection. When parents are physically or emotionally absent, their children feel a need to know they are loved. Often love and sex are blurred together in their minds, and they use sex to satisfy their longing for love.[16]

In homes where parental influence is strong, adolescents are less likely to become pregnant. Involved parents generally encourage their teens toward positive behaviors and discourage them from sexual activity. They provide modeling and motivation for abstinence from sex outside marriage.[17]

Even without strong input from parents, even in an environment filled with sexual suggestion, not every teenage girl becomes pregnant. Not every teenager is sexually active. Whether a girl has sex and whether she becomes pregnant is a complex web of many factors.

Chapter 3

Why Teens Become Pregnant

When she was fourteen, Sandra did not like herself. However, she escaped her feelings of worthlessness by going to parties. At parties, guys paid attention to her, older guys, and that made her feel good. Some of them also loaded her up with drugs and drinks. She did not think about sex, pregnancy, or birth control. All she cared about was feeling good.

"At fourteen," she said, three years later, "I didn't know that what I did was sex. Because of the drinking and the drugs, I didn't realize I was pregnant. When I finally figured it out, my mother cried. She didn't yell; she just cried. My father wouldn't talk to me until I went in the hospital to have the baby."

Sandra's parents had her baby's nineteen-year-old father put in jail for statutory rape. Statutory rape occurs when someone eighteen or older has sex with a person under a certain age. This age is different, depending on the state where the act was committed. Even if the sex was not forced, it is still considered statutory rape if the minor was under a certain age.

Sandra and her little boy live with her parents. "Being a mother is stressful," she admits. "I have to wake up earlier than usual so I can feed him and get him dressed. After school, he's all mine. He doesn't go to bed until 11:00 at night."

Sandra cries when she thinks about the friends she used to pal around with. "My friends don't want to deal with it [her responsibilities as a mother]. I don't have any friends."[1]

Sandra's pregnancy was the result of a number of factors. Low self-esteem, the decision to hang out with people who were much older than she, the choice to drink and do drugs, lack of knowledge about birth control—all these played parts. Teenagers become pregnant for many different reasons.

Low Self-esteem

One factor that is frequently connected with teen pregnancy is low self-esteem.[2] When a girl does not feel good about herself, she often looks to other people to tell her she has value. Having a boyfriend can make her feel attractive, and the older the boy is who likes her, the better she feels about herself. Sometimes girls have sex just to keep a boyfriend, because being with a boy gives her a sense of worth.

Having a baby gives some girls a feeling of importance they do not have otherwise. Some say, "Now I'll have someone to love me." For teenage boys, too, having a child can raise the image they or others have of them. Fathering a child may make them feel as though they are "real men."

Resisting the pressure to have sex, which is so common among adolescents, is harder for teens who do not feel good about themselves. How do young people who do not trust their own decision-making abilities act when all their friends

*S*ome teens mistakenly believe that having a baby will make them seem more important than they are. They do not realize all the work and self-sacrifice involved in raising a child.

are having sex or when being a virgin is looked on as shameful? How can they say no when those they think of as smarter, more popular, and more successful say yes so easily? A young girl's sense of self-worth affects whether the choices she makes will be what she really wants or what others expect from her.

Sexual Abuse

The self-esteem and the self-expectations of some adolescents have been twisted by sexual abuse they experienced as children or teenagers. When young people have sex forced on them, they usually feel guilty or ashamed. Even though others have bullied, tricked, or frightened them into sexual activity, children are often told that they were to blame for the touching or the intercourse. They become conditioned to believe that they deserve to be taken advantage of sexually. They may feel they have already given away their virginity, even though it was, in reality, taken from them. They have little reason to say no. Even when the molestation occurred years earlier, teens who were abused often think they have no reason to refuse sex because they are already "stained."[3]

Abused girls may also have learned that having sex is supposed to be an expression of affection. So when they look for someone to love and value them, they think of sex as part of that relationship. Saying no to sex would be, for them, saying no to a chance for love and happiness. This warped view of love and the great damage to a child's self-image caused by sexual mistreatment make abused girls especially vulnerable to sexual suggestion. Possibly well over half of all teen mothers were sexually abused as children.[4]

Drinking and Drugs

Low self-esteem and childhood sexual abuse contribute strongly but indirectly to teen pregnancy. The lifestyle choices adolescents make have direct influence on their chances of becoming teen parents. Those who choose to drink, take drugs, and party with older friends tend to become pregnant early. Alcohol is involved in about one fourth of all adolescent intercourse.[5]

Drugs, whether stimulants or depressants, and alcohol lower the ability to think clearly. The more alcohol and drugs people consume, the less they are able to control their physical and emotional urges. Teens who get drunk or high have difficulty considering the potential consequences of their actions. They may begin by watching a suggestive video or simply by flirting. Sexual thoughts and flirting may lead to touching or kissing. Touching and kissing generally lead to more serious petting, and heavy petting can lead to sexual intercourse. At any point, either the boy or girl can stop. But when people cannot think clearly, they do not see how one step leads to another. They may not stop the action. Drugs and alcohol make it hard to interrupt this train of events.

*C*armen Ford (left) of the National Campaign to Prevent Teen Pregnancy answers questions about preventing teen pregnancy and AIDS during a conference in Washington, D.C., in 1997. Ford is joined by actress Lark Voorhies (center) and DaJour (right), the host of *Teen Summit* on Black Entertainment Television.

Self-control is even more difficult when nearly everyone around is older. Adolescents, particularly those with low self-esteem, want to be seen as grown-up. Hanging out with older friends is one way of feeling more adult. Doing the things older people do is a way of appearing grown-up. So when older friends are drinking or having sex, doing the same is often more important than avoiding the possible consequences.

Invincibility Myth

In the minds of most teenagers, there are no bad consequences, at least not for them. Adolescents commonly believe that they are invincible—that nothing terribly bad can ever happen to them. They think they will live forever.[6] Their best friends could have been in car accidents, acquired sexually transmitted diseases, or become pregnant, but they cannot imagine they would ever have to face such problems.

Failure to Use Birth Control Effectively

So some teens do not use contraception. Contraception, or birth control, is something that makes getting pregnant less likely to occur. Some teens have completely mistaken ideas about how they can or cannot get pregnant. They think pregnancy is impossible if they have sex standing up, if they douche (clean themselves) afterward with certain products, or if it is their first time. The truth is that 20 percent of all teenagers get pregnant the first time they have sex.[7]

Those whose families have higher incomes and those with higher academic goals use contraception more often than poorer, less motivated youth.[8] The reason is not entirely access—birth control is available without charge and without question at many clinics and family-planning agencies. Some less educated teens may not be aware of the free services or have know how to obtain them, but a large number of low-income teens get contraceptives from family-planning clinics.[9] The reason poorer teens do not use birth control as frequently as others may be that they have less incentive to avoid pregnancy. They generally do not have the kinds of goals and options that having babies would hinder. Many live in communities that are very accepting of early childbirth and supportive of young parents.[10]

Despite the availability of contraceptives to

Reasons Teens Give for Not Using Birth Control

✓ I did not like it.

✓ It did not feel comfortable.

✓ I was embarrassed.

✓ I thought it would make me sterile.

✓ He said he was sterile.

✓ I kept telling myself I could wait a little bit longer.

✓ I ran out of pills.

✓ I forgot.

✓ I thought we were careful enough.

✓ She told me she was on the pill.

✓ I did not think I could get pregnant.

young people, one out of four teens who has sex does not use any protection against pregnancy.[11] Naturally, those who do not use protection are the most likely to become pregnant. Nearly three fourths of all teen pregnancies occur to young women who are not using birth control.[12]

But the adolescents who do not use birth control are not the only ones having babies. A quarter of a million teens use contraception but still get pregnant. The method they are using may fail, or they may fail to use the method correctly. Any form of birth control can be ineffective if the people using it

➤ are inexperienced and do not use it correctly;

➤ are immature and do not use it carefully; or

➢ are forgetful or irresponsible and do not use it consistently.

Just as contraceptive use is lower among lower-income groups, failure of birth control is higher—about twice as high—among poor teens.[13]

The choice of contraceptive method also affects the possibility of failure. Average failure rates range from 21 percent for foams and gels to 3 percent for the Pill.[14] The Pill is a form of birth control that is taken orally by a woman on a regular basis. Sixty-five percent of girls having sex for the first time choose condoms to prevent both pregnancy and sexually transmitted disease. Then as they become more experienced or more comfortable in a relationship, more begin using the Pill.[15] The contraceptives used most frequently by teenagers are

➢ the Pill, the most effective at preventing pregnancy, used by 44 percent;

➢ condoms, the most effective at preventing sexually transmitted diseases, used by 38 percent;

➢ injections, similar to the Pill in shot form, 10 percent;

➢ withdrawal, pulling the penis out before intercourse is completed, 4 percent; and

➢ implant, inserted under the skin of the arm, 3 percent.[16]

When birth control fails, for whatever reason, both mother and father face a new set of choices.

Chapter 4

Choices for Pregnant Teens

Ever since Brenda began having sex with Claude, she worried about getting pregnant. Claude did not like to use condoms, and Brenda did not insist. Finally, it happened. Just a few months before she was to graduate from high school, Brenda learned that she was pregnant.

Claude said he would marry her, but Brenda was not sure she wanted to spend the rest of her life with him. She thought about abortion but did not feel right about it. She made arrangements to give birth and allow her baby to be adopted. But when the tiny boy was placed in her arms, she struggled with her decision. She wrote in her journal: "Adoption is brave . . . painful, scary, 'best' for you and me. It means freedom. . . . Keeping is emotional . . . foolish . . . love-filled. . . . It means responsibility. . . . Am I really ready for this?" She chose to keep her son and raise him alone.

A difficult year later, she visited Claude and got pregnant again. This time, she did not think twice. She did not want to face the emotional seesaw of loving a child and having to care for it. This time she had an abortion.[1]

Every girl who gets pregnant faces the same choices as Brenda. Should she abort or give birth? If she chooses to give birth, should she let the baby be adopted or should she raise the child herself? If she chooses to raise her child, should she marry or remain single? Every option involves some gain and some loss.

Birth or Abortion

The 1973 *Roe* v. *Wade* Supreme Court decision made abortion legal throughout the United States. In the previous year, about 75 percent of all pregnant teens gave birth. The other 25 percent either had miscarriages or illegal abortions. After the court ruling, only 50 percent gave birth.[2] Many girls opted for abortion. In 1996, 274,000 abortions were performed on teenagers.[3]

Abortion is more likely to be selected by girls with higher family incomes, higher school achievement, and higher career goals. About 75 percent of affluent girls with unintended pregnancies seek abortions. These teens usually have parents who have the money and the willingness to end their daughters' pregnancies. Among poorer girls, however, less than half attempt to terminate their unplanned pregnancies. Sixty percent of white teens and less than 50 percent of African-American and Hispanic adolescents seek abortions.[4]

Abortion solves the immediate problem of an unwanted pregnancy, but it can create other difficulties. Although the procedure is normally very safe, any surgery has risks. In a few cases, abortions have caused excessive bleeding, damage to the cervix, and other medical complications. The chances of future miscarriage are greatly increased with each abortion performed.[5] For some, the psychological trauma can be very deep and long lasting. Many girls who undergo abortions feel guilt and depression, at least briefly, some for months or years.[6] The later in the pregnancy the abortion is performed, the greater the possibility and severity of negative effects.

If a teenage girl decides to give birth, she can take steps to help ensure a healthy delivery and a healthy baby. A nutritious diet allows a baby to grow properly. A pregnant woman needs good food,

*T*wo teenage mothers spend time with their babies at a county funded day-care center at their high school in Minneapolis. The young mothers are two of twenty-eight students who drop off their toddlers at the center so that they can finish school.

plenty of water, and usually, extra iron and vitamins. Moderate physical exercise and sufficient sleep give the mother's body strength and energy. These will be needed when it is time to give birth.[7]

Some substances can harm both mother and baby. Cigarettes should be avoided because smoking has been linked to very serious problems. Pregnant women who smoke have more miscarriages and premature deliveries. When a mother smokes, her blood vessels narrow, so her baby gets less oxygen and nutrients. Babies of smokers are more likely to be underweight, sickly, and prone to Sudden Infant Death Syndrome (crib death).[8]

Alcohol also causes serious harm to mother and baby. Mothers who drink increase their chances of bleeding, miscarrying, or delivering too early. Their babies can be born with Fetal Alcohol Syndrome, which means one or more of several problems: They may develop slowly physically, mentally, or psychologically. Their heads, faces, arms, and legs may not be shaped normally. They may have problems with their hearts or kidneys. They may be hyperactive, have learning disabilities, or have behavior problems. Drinking during pregnancy is the third leading cause of mental retardation among children in the United States.[9]

Like tobacco and alcohol, other drugs should not be taken during pregnancy. Marijuana, cocaine, heroin, and amphetamines can have the same disastrous effects as smoking and drinking. Even the drugs that are in medicines can be harmful. To be safe, pregnant women should talk with their doctors before taking any medication.[10]

Seeing a doctor is one of the most important things a pregnant woman can do. A good doctor observes the progress of the pregnancy and teaches the mother how to keep herself and her baby as healthy as possible. Women who do not go regularly to the doctor or who do not go early in their pregnancy risk having a baby with health problems. One third of pregnant teens do not receive proper prenatal medical care.[11]

Adoption or Keeping a Child

If the decision is to give birth, the next question is: Who will raise the child? Overwhelmingly, teens are answering, "I will." More than 70 percent of white teenage girls and 90 percent of African-American teenage girls are choosing to keep their babies.[12] Very few are offering their infants up for adoption.

As Brenda wrote, adoption may be the best arrangement for both parent and child. Adopted children are generally placed in homes where they are desperately wanted and where good finances can provide them many material advantages. Teens who choose adoption are freed from a responsibility they are not able to handle.

But with the gain comes tremendous loss. Teens who give their babies up lose the child they had begun to love. They lose part of their own flesh and blood. They sometimes feel cheated out of the product of nine months of pregnancy.[13]

The choice to keep the baby is also a mixture of gain and loss. On the plus side is a new life with its unlimited potential. On the negative side are the daily responsibilities for nurturing that new life.

Marriage or Single Parent

Those responsibilities are especially difficult when they are shouldered alone. Yet less than half of all unwed adolescent parents marry within ten years after having a baby.[14] A few live independently, with only their children. A small number live in group homes or shelters. Most live with their parents or their boyfriends' families.

Choosing marriage has advantages for mother and child. Marriage provides someone to share in the work, costs, decisions, and emotions of parenting. The presence of a father as well as a mother gives a child additional love, time, and attention, and a male role model.[15]

Early marriage has disadvantages also. Young men may be too immature to parent well and take more of their wives' time and energy than they contribute. If only one partner brings in an income, that person may resent the other. The daily demands of caring for children may create stress and unhappiness in the marriage. Sometimes when people marry young, they try later to recapture the youth they feel they missed, and they do not remain faithful to their partner. When a man marries to give his baby a father, his wife often questions his love for her. She does not have the security she may have sought in marriage.[16]

Just as the decision to have sex leads to other choices that must be made, the decision to keep and raise a child brings with it another set of circumstances that must be faced.

Chapter 5

The Consequences of Teen Pregnancy

Scott started having sex when he was in the eighth grade. By the time he got to high school, he was already a father. When he heard the news, his attitude was, "If you're man enough to have sex, be man enough to take care of what's yours. I was man enough to make it; I'm going to be man enough to support it all my life."

Today, at twenty-three, Scott works sixteen hours a day. He goes to his first job at eight in the morning and finishes his second at midnight. If his child is awake when he gets home, he takes care of her until two or three in the morning. He gets five or six hours of sleep every night. He has no time for anyone outside his little family. But, he says, in the long run he's going to be successful.[1]

Not every teen father is like Scott. Some abandon their girlfriends, their children, and all the obligations that come with making a baby. Not every teen mother is responsible. Some thrust their children on their parents or others and go on as though the births had not happened. But teenage childbirth does happen to more than half a million teenage girls every year, and the consequences are great—for the fathers, the mothers, the children, and society.

For Fathers

The majority of males who father children by teenage mothers do not stay involved long in their children's lives physically or financially. Although some teenage fathers may say they want to help their girlfriends during pregnancy and participate in raising their children, one third of the children of unmarried parents (and most teens are unmarried) never see their fathers.[2]

When a father's physical presence is missing, his financial help is often absent, too. In an attempt to force fathers to contribute to their children's support, Congress passed the Family Support Act in 1988. The law requires that paternity be established for all children—that the father be identified even if he is not married to the mother. Then the amount of support the father must pay is determined on the basis of his income, and his employer takes the payment directly from his paychecks. The father continues to pay until his child is eighteen years old.

A number of fathers voluntarily take on the responsibility of supporting their families. Sometimes they do not live with their children and their children's mother because the mother may be able to get welfare or other benefits only if she is a single parent.[3] For fathers who choose to support their children, earning enough money is often difficult. The 80 percent of teen parents who were poor before their children were conceived have few jobs open to them after the babies are born. Even though

*S*ome young fathers take responsibility for their children, working extra hours to afford food, clothing, and health care for their families.

the fathers are likely to be in their early twenties, they are generally unskilled, undereducated, and living in communities where little work is available. Even when the age of the fathers is the same, fathers of babies born to teen mothers earn less than half (38 percent) of what fathers of babies born to nonteen mothers earn.[4]

Because these responsible fathers typically work at low-paying jobs, they must work long hours to make enough money to support their babies and their babies' mothers. Working long hours does not give them time to get more education or training. In fact, less than half (39 percent) even graduate from high school.[5] Without better education, they cannot find better-paying jobs. Dropping out of school to support a family can trap fathers and their children in a lifetime of poverty.

For Mothers

The same seemingly inescapable circle traps mothers as well, whether or not their babies' fathers support them. Poor surroundings and incomplete education offer them only low-paying jobs. Earning low pay forces them to drop out of school. Dropping out of school holds them in low-paying jobs, and low-paying jobs keep them in poverty. Most teen moms (84 percent) receive some form of public assistance (welfare) at some time. Three in ten go on welfare within three years after the birth of their first child.[6] More than four in ten are still living in poverty at age twenty-seven.[7]

The situation is worsened by the fact that teen mothers tend to have larger families. One in four teens gets pregnant a second time within two years after her first child is born.[8] Girls who begin childbearing in their teens generally have one to two more children than those who wait.[9]

Often the mother is a single parent for a long time. This means that, in addition to the often impossible task of finding employment that will support two and sometimes more, she must deal with the problem of child care. Unless relatives or friends are available and willing to help, she typically pays one fourth of her small income for child care, just to be able to work.[10]

Affordability is only one issue in child care. Since only half of all teen mothers complete high school,[11] and many of those have low-skill equivalency certification rather than diplomas, the types of jobs

*T*his baby was born addicted to the drugs her mother took during pregnancy. The infant must stay in a dark room, protected from bright lights and loud noises that would overstimulate her.

open to adolescent mothers are usually in retail stores or restaurants. These jobs require employees to work evenings and weekends. Child care is difficult to find at these times. Nearly every child-care center refuses to care for children who are even slightly sick, so mothers miss days of work when their children are ill.

For Children

The children of teenage mothers are ill more often and more seriously than the children of older mothers.[12] They are more likely to have been born prematurely and underweight, largely because their mothers do not obtain proper prenatal care. Some teen mothers put off getting medical attention until their pregnancies are well advanced, and some do not have health insurance. Babies that are born either too early or too small are more fragile and catch diseases more easily than others. They may not have developed completely before birth, so they have medical or developmental conditions that are with them for years, sometimes for life.

Children of teen parents have not only health problems, but also greater difficulty in school. They tend to score lower on tests of ability and achievement. They are more likely to have to repeat grades. Sometimes their behavior is poor and they have a hard time controlling themselves. These school-related problems are probably not due to the fact that their mothers were young, but that most of their mothers are poor, single, and not well educated.[13] Such mothers have fewer resources to give their children. They do not have as many books for their children to read. They do not have transportation or money for enriching experiences. They cannot help their children with difficult homework.

Whether because teen mothers also have fewer emotional resources or because some have inadequate parental role models, children of adolescents are abused and neglected more often than other children. Children born to mothers under the age of eighteen are one and a half times (150 percent) more likely to be mistreated or ignored than children born to older parents.[14]

That abuse or neglect, especially when coupled with the disadvantages of poverty, sometimes results in anger, behavioral problems, and even crime in the children of teen parents. Of all the men in prisons between fifteen and nineteen years of age, 90 percent were born to teen mothers.[15] More than 10 percent of the children of teenagers serve some time in jail or prison, a rate 2.7 times higher than for any other group.[16]

A significant number of daughters of teen moms repeat the pattern of early pregnancy set by their mothers.[17] Most second-generation childbirths result from the same set of circumstances that gave rise to the parent's pregnancy—poverty, few role models of anything different, no other expectations, no dreams for anything else.

Regardless of the reasons, every pregnancy costs something. For teenage pregnancies, much of the financial cost is often paid not by the teenagers, but by people they do not even know.

For Society

Out-of-wedlock births to teens cost national, state, and local governments billions of dollars every year. These costs are borne by those who pay taxes.[18] The

Estimated Yearly Costs to Taxpayers of Teenage Childbearing

Public assistance

Aid to Families with Dependent Children (AFDC) benefits	$2.1 billion
Food stamps	1.2 billion
Rent subsidies	0.8 billion
Medical aid for teen parents	0.8 billion
Medical aid for children	1.3 billion
Administrative costs	0.5 billion
Total public assistance	**$6.7 billion**

Tax losses

From mother's lower income	$3.2 billion
From father's lower income	2.6 billion
Total tax losses	**$5.8 billion**

Treatment of problems as children grow

Foster care	$1.7 billion
Imprisonment	5.2 billion
Tax losses (from unemployed young adult children)	1.3 billion
Total treatment	**$8.2 billion**
Total cost	**$20.7 billion**

Source: Rebecca A. Maynard, ed., *Kids Having Kids: Economic Costs and Social Consequences of Teen Pregnancy* (Washington, D.C.: Urban Institute, 1997), p. 309.

cost of feeding, clothing, sheltering, and educating children is high, as is medical care. The majority of adolescent parents do not make enough money to care for the needs of their babies. Mothers and fathers who drop out of school to support their families usually find their incomes unable to keep up with the needs of their growing children. Therefore, "society"—taxpayers—pay a good share of those expenses.

In addition to the costs of raising children, teen childbearing places other financial burdens on the public. The abuse that is higher in families begun by adolescents adds costs for social workers and foster care. The higher involvement of teens' children in crime adds costs for construction and maintenance of prisons. The lower income of teen parents and, later, of their children, reduces tax revenues.

Teen childbearing has serious consequences for the parents, for the children, and for society. To avoid those consequences, the trends must be changed.

Chapter 6

Changing the Trends

Claudia used to cry whenever she told her story. She told it to anyone who would listen. She spoke to adults who might be interested in helping teen moms. She spoke to classrooms of junior-high students, encouraging them to avoid the pain she had suffered. Everyone thought she was so lucky to be living by herself in an apartment.

"You don't understand," she would tell them through her tears. "You don't understand how lonely it is." She tried to make them understand. "My baby's father promised me the sun, moon, and stars," she said. "But when I told him I was pregnant, he was gone."

Claudia had lived with her mother, but her mother sent her to her father when Claudia became pregnant. She stayed with him a few months. Then, after the baby came, her father kicked her out, too. Going to school, working, and then coming home to an apartment with just her baby, Diego—it was all very hard. She had no one to talk to, no one to care.

But her teacher cared and matched her up with a mentor who wanted to be a friend to a teen mom and her baby. Sandy was totally different from Claudia. She was educated and well-dressed and carried herself confidently. But Claudia could tell she was interested in her, and little by little, she opened up to her new friend. Sandy encouraged Claudia in her studies, gave her advice about Diego, and met her often for lunch. Mostly she listened and helped Claudia to dream about her future. Sandy introduced her to a neighbor, who hired Claudia to work in her accounting business.

Today Claudia is a very valuable employee in that company. She has nearly finished college, and her boss hopes she will stay with the firm. Diego is doing well, and Claudia no longer cries when she tells her story.[1]

Claudia was a typical pregnant teen. From a low-income minority family, she was raised in a single-parent home. No one in her family had finished high school, and no one expected Claudia to do any better. She was flattered by the attentions of an older guy and believed what he told her. But Claudia is no longer a statistic. She is breaking the cycle of poverty and dependency for herself and her son.

The problem of teen pregnancy, the trend toward more and more unmarried teens having babies at increasingly younger ages, can be stopped. Even if the trend is not stopped completely, its negative consequences can be diminished.

Preventing Pregnancy

The first step in reversing the tide is pregnancy prevention. There are certain things every teen, male and female, should seriously consider to keep from becoming pregnant or getting someone pregnant.

*T*his billboard in downtown Baltimore displays a message of abstinence. Abstinence is the only sure way to prevent teen pregnancy, or pregnancy of any kind for that matter.

Deciding on limits to sex. To keep from getting pregnant, teens must realize that having sex, even with contraception, always carries the risk of pregnancy. They must decide when they would be willing to take that risk. At a certain age? When married? When some goal such as graduation from high school or college has been achieved? The only certain way to not get pregnant is to not have sex.

If adolescents choose not to have sex, they can set limits on what they will do and what they will allow others to do to them physically. A kiss can lead to a touch, which can lead to more intimate contact. Deciding where to draw the line ahead of time, when no emotions are involved, makes it easier to

Contraceptive Choices

Method	How It Works	Effectiveness	Advantages	Disadvantages
Abstinence	Couple does not have sex	100%	No health risks.	No disadvantages.
Implants	Tubes placed under the skin in the upper arm release substance that stops eggs from leaving the ovaries	99%	Work for 5 years. Do not interfere with intercourse.	Changes in periods. Do not prevent STDs.
Shots (Depo-Provera)	Shot every 12 weeks prevents egg from leaving ovaries	99%	Work for 12 weeks. Do not interfere with intercourse.	Changes in periods. Possible nausea, sore breasts, weight gain, mood changes. Do not prevent STDs.
Pill	Prevents fertilization of woman's egg	95-99%	Does not interfere with intercourse. Protects against certain cancers and other medical problems.	Needs to be taken according to strict schedule. Possible weight gain and other slight physical problems. Possible link to later breast cancer. Does not prevent STDs.
Condom	Sheath worn over the penis to prevent sperm from entering the female	85-97% Combination with spermicide increases effectiveness	Protects against STDs. Prescription not needed. Easy to carry.	Interrupts sex. May reduce sexual pleasure. Can break or come off.
IUD	Device inserted into uterus that prevents fertilized egg from implanting in uterus	94-98%	Does not interrupt intercourse.	Insertion may be painful. Risk of infections that can lead to infertility. Can be pushed out without user's awareness. Does not prevent STDs.

Contraceptive Choices

Method	How It Works	Effectiveness	Advantages	Disadvantages
Diaphragm	Cup fits over the cervix to block sperm—used with spermicide	82%	Can be put in 6 hours before intercourse. Not felt during intercourse.	Must be left in for 6-8 hours after intercourse. May cause bladder infections. Must be fitted by doctor. Does not prevent STDs.
Cervical cap	Cup placed inside the vagina over the cervix to block sperm—used with spermicide	82% for women who have not had children, 64% for others	Can be put in several hours before intercourse. Not felt during intercourse.	Can injure cervical tissue. Can be difficult to insert.
Spermicides (foam, cream, gel, suppository)	Chemicals placed deep in vagina just before intercourse kill sperm	75-80%	Some protection against STDs. Adds lubrication. Available without prescription.	Interrupts intercourse. Can be messy. Some may irritate vagina or penis.
Female condom	Thin cone with two rings—one goes inside the vagina and one outside—keeping sperm from the egg	79%	Also protects against STDs. Does not need to interrupt intercourse. Available without prescription.	Some people dislike the outer ring.
Withdrawal	Man withdraws his penis from the vagina before he climaxes.	Very low.	None.	Can still result in pregnancy. (Some fluid comes out of the penis before the man actually climaxes.) Does not prevent STDs.

Sources: *Your Contraceptive Choices for Now, for Later,* U.S. Department of Health and Human Services, Public Health Service, Bethesda, Md., 1989; *What is Right for You? Choosing a Birth Control Method,* Education Program Associates, Campbell, Calif., 1994; Interview with Planned Parenthood members.

carry out that decision even when feelings and sensations are aroused.

If the choice is made to have sex, birth control is essential for avoiding pregnancy. People deciding to have sex should figure out ahead of time which contraceptive method is best for them. They should learn how to use it and decide to use it every time they have sex. Whatever method of birth control is selected, the use of condoms also will help protect against sexually transmitted disease. Some contraceptives have a higher success rate than others, but none is 100 percent foolproof. Every time two people have sex, the female risks getting pregnant and both often risk getting a disease.

Avoiding risky behaviors. Alcohol and drugs hinder clear thinking. They can make self-control difficult. People wanting to keep from getting pregnant should keep away from alcohol and drugs and from places where having sex seems to be expected.

Choice of friends also affects pregnancy risk. Older friends sometimes encourage young teens to have sex. Younger teens often want to appear older to please their friends and may have difficulty saying no.

Building self-esteem. People who feel good about themselves are more able to act responsibly.[2] A healthy self-concept helps young people avoid the risky behaviors that lead to pregnancy. Every person has great value. Every teen is important.

Setting goals. Teens with high expectations for themselves have lower rates of sexual activity.[3] Keeping long-term life goals in mind can help teens avoid the situations that would jeopardize those goals. Pregnancy affects many adolescent dreams.

Finding a trustworthy adult friend. When questions and situations are too difficult for a teen, an adult can help. Adults can be role models, can listen, can even offer advice. Adults have many more years of experience than teenagers. Sometimes young people think no one understands or cares about them, but many adults care and are willing to help. Good parents are very often the best adult friends. Other adult friends might be teachers, coaches, or recreation leaders. In some communities, mentoring programs match teens with understanding adult mentors. A trusted adult can help a teenager through the difficulties of adolescence.

Overcoming the Odds

If a teenage girl gets pregnant and decides to have the baby, she can turn what could be a negative into a positive. If a young man discovers he is to be a father, he can become a great father. Here are some things teenagers can do to take charge of their situations and make good lives for themselves and their families:

Get prenatal care for the mother. Most of the health problems in children of teen moms result from the mother's failure to see a doctor early in her pregnancy. Getting medical attention and following the doctor's instructions will increase the chances for a healthy baby. Many clinics provide prenatal care at little or no cost. Some are listed in the phone book's yellow pages under *family planning*.

Stay in school. Some schools have programs for teen parents that include nursery care for children. School guidance counselors usually know how to get into these programs. No matter how long it takes

*T*hese three high school students are part of a class designed to discourage unwanted teenage pregnancy. Their individual *Baby Think It Over Dolls* cry periodically to teach students one of the realities of parenting.

to graduate or how hard it is to get a high school diploma, that diploma is a ticket to a better-paying job. A college diploma opens the door to even more and better jobs. The more education parents get, the better jobs they will be able to find and the more they will have to give their children.

Find resources for children. Libraries, schools, churches, clubs, and recreation centers have materials that will enrich children. Books, music, educational television shows, athletic programs, and other activities stimulate mental and social development. The more good experiences parents and children have, the more possibilities are opened up for a brighter future.

Keep good goals in mind. The dreams parents have for themselves and their children keep them going when they feel tired or discouraged. For every goal, parents can write down the little steps necessary to reach the final aim. They can check off each step as it is accomplished.

Hook up with an adult friend. Whether a parent or another mentor, an older friend can encourage teen parents, give them practical help, and keep them on track. An adult friend can share with a teen the difficulties and the joys of parenting. A school guidance counselor, a rabbi, or a minister may be helpful in finding a mentor.

Setting a New Course

Some of the blame for the teen pregnancy problem can be placed on adults. Adults are largely responsible for creating the highly sexual, permissive environment in which adolescents grow up. Much of the blame falls on teens as a result of the choices they make. In some ways, teen pregnancy is everyone's concern. Doctors and nurses treat the young mothers and their babies. Teachers educate the children born to half a million teenage mothers each year. Social service agencies provide food, clothing, and other support to many teen parents and their families. Taxpayers fund school nurseries and other programs created by teen pregnancy.

But reversing the trends can be accomplished only by teenagers. Adults can create programs, provide education, give discipline, and set examples. But the decisions to have sex or abstain, to use contraception or not, to raise a child—these decisions are made by individual young people. The direction of teen pregnancy in the United States will depend on the decisions of its teenagers.

Organizations

Child Welfare League of America
440 First Street, NW, Third Floor
Washington, DC 20001-2085
(202) 638-2952
<http://www.cwla.org/>

Common Ground Network for Life and Choice
1601 Connecticut Ave., NW, Suite 200
Washington, DC 20009
(202) 265-4300
<http://www.journalism.wisc.edu/cpn/
common_ground/>

March of Dimes Birth Defects Foundation
1275 Mamaroneck Avenue
White Plains, NY 10605
(888) 663-4637
<http://www.modimes.org/>

The National Women's Health Information Center (NWHIC)
(800) 994-9662
<http://www.4women.gov>

A number of local organizations offer mentors, counseling, and group activities and programs for teens. Some of these people and programs help teens to prevent pregnancy, some help teens who are pregnant or parenting, and some do both. These include

➢ youth organizations, such as the YMCA and the YWCA

➢ recreation programs, such as Boys and Girls Clubs

➢ social service organizations

➢ family planning agencies

➢ colleges

➢ churches

➢ hospitals

For More Information

State, county, and city government agencies also have programs under the headings *Health*, *Adolescents*, and *Social Services* in your local phone book.

Web Sites

The Alan Guttmacher Institute: Teen Sex and Pregnancy
<http://www.agi-usa.org/pubs/fb_teen_sex.html>

Centers for Disease Control and Prevention (CDC): Teen Pregnancy
<http://www.cdc.gov/nccdphp/teen.htm>

Office of Population Affairs: Trends in Adolescent Pregnancy and Childbearing
<http://www.hhs.gov/progorg/opa/pregtrnd.html>

Chapter 1. The Problem of Teen Pregnancy

1. Personal interview, spring 1997.

2. Rebecca A. Maynard, ed., *Kids Having Kids: Economic Costs and Social Consequences of Teen Pregnancy* (Washington, D.C.: Urban Institute, 1997), p. 1.

3. Ibid.

4. U.S. Census Bureau, Statistical Abstract (Washington, D.C.: U.S. Government Printing Office, 1998), table 91.

5. Alison M. Spitz, et. al., "Pregnancy, Abortion, and Birth Rates Among U.S. Adolescents—1980, 1985, and 1990," *Journal of the American Medical Association* 275, April 3, 1999, pp. 989–993.

6. Iris F. Litt, "Pregnancy in Adolescence," *Journal of the American Medical Association* 275, April 3, 1995, p. 1030.

7. Maynard, p. 25.

8. March of Dimes Birth Defects Foundation, *Teenage Pregnancy: Facts You Should Know*, n.d., <http://babynet.ddwi.com/tlc/pregnancy/teenfact.html> January 1999.

9. Kristin Luker, *Dubious Conceptions: The Politics of Teenage Pregnancy* (Cambridge, Mass.: Harvard University Press, 1996), p. 110.

10. K.A. Moore, B.C. Miller, D. Glei, and D.R. Morrison, *Early Sex, Contraception, and Childbearing: A Review of Recent Research* (Washington, D.C.: Child Trends, 1995).

11. Alan Guttmacher Institute, *Sex and America's Teenagers* (New York: Alan Guttmacher Institute, 1994), p. 82.

12. Maynard, p. 64.

13. Dr. Claire Brindis, in Harriet Chiang, "Why Children Have Children," *San Francisco Chronicle*, March 8, 1998, Sunday section, p. 4.

14. Irwin Garfinkel and Sara McLanahan, *Single Mothers and Their Children: A New American Dilemma* (Washington, D.C.: Urban Institute, 1986).

15. B.L. Devaney and K.S. Hubley, "The Determinants of Adolescent Pregnancy and Childbearing," Report of the National Institute of Child Health and Human Development, *U.S. Department of Health and Human Services* (Washington, D.C.: U.S. Government Printing Office, 1981).

16. Brindis, p. 4.

17. Mike A. Males, *The Scapegoat Generation* (Monroe, Maine: Common Courage Press, 1996), p. 17.

18. Joe Klein, "The Predator Problem," *Newsweek*, April 29, 1996, p. 32.

Chapter 2. Teens at Risk

1. Personal contacts, 1984–1997.

2. Peggy Clarke, "Teen-Age Sex Survey Would Teach Risks," *The New York Times*, August 7, 1991, p. A20.

3. American Social Health Association, "Trends in *Sexual Risk Behavior Among High School Students—United States*, 1990, 1991, and 1993," *MMWR* 1995: 44, pp. 124–131.

4. Rebecca A. Maynard, ed., *Kids Having Kids: Economic Costs and Social Consequences of Teen Pregnancy* (Washington, D.C.: Urban Institute, 1997), p. 32.

5. S. Robert Lichter, Linda S. Lichter, and Stanley Rothman, *Watching America* (New York: HarperCollins, 1991), p. 26.

6. Barry S. Sapolsky and Joseph O. Tabarlet, "Sex in Primetime Television: 1979 versus 1989," *Journal of Broadcasting and Electronic Media* 15, no. 4, fall 1991, p. 514.

7. V.C. Strasburger, *Adolescents and the Media: Medical and Psychological Impact* (Newbury Park, Calif.: Sage, 1995), cited in Carnegie Council on Adolescent Development, *Great Transitions: Preparing Adolescents for a New Century* (New York: Carnegie Corporation of New York, 1995), p. 115.

8. Walt Mueller, *Understanding Today's Youth Culture* (Wheaton, Ill.: Tyndale House, 1994), p. 132.

9. Quentin J. Schultze et al., *Dancing in the Dark* (Grand Rapids, Mich.: Wm. B. Eerdmans, 1991), p. 222.

10. Kim Neely, "Homestyle," *Rolling Stone*, February 4, 1993, p. 34.

11. American Academy of Pediatrics, "Sexuality, Contraception, and the Media," *Pediatrics* 95, no. 2, February 1995, pp. 298–300.

12. From *Sassy*, cited in Mueller, p. 154.

13. Mueller, p. 131

14. "Teenagers," Barna Research Online, 1994, <http://www.barna.org/cgi-bin/PageCategory.asp?CategoryID=37> (October 28, 1999).

15. Mueller, p. 214.

16. David Popenoe, *Life Without Father* (New York: Martin Kessler, 1996), p. 159.

17. F. Philip Rice, *The Adolescent: Development, Relationships, and Culture*, 11th ed. (Boston: Allyn and Bacon, 1992), pp. 371–372.

Chapter 3. Why Teens Become Pregnant

1. Sandra Ramirex, presentation at Teen and Parent Forum, sponsored by Valley Children's Hospital, Fresno, Calif., September 12, 1998.

2. F. Philip Rice, *The Adolescent: Development, Relationships, and Culture*, 11th ed. (Boston: Allyn and Bacon, 1992), p. 248.

3. Bryan Strong and Christine DeVault, *The Marriage and Family Experience*, 6th ed. (Minneapolis: West, 1995), pp. 516–518.

4. Rebecca A. Maynard, ed., *Kids Having Kids: Economic Costs and Social Consequences of Teen Pregnancy* (Washington, D.C.: Urban Institute, 1997), p. 4.

5. B.H. Jacobson, S.G. Aldana, and T. Beaty, "Adolescent Sexual Behavior and Associated Variables," *Journal of Health Education* 25, no. 1, 1994, pp. 10–12.

6. Rice, p. 211.

7. Dr. Claire Brindis, cited in Ken Robinson, "Valley Is Hotbed of 'Danger Factors,'" *Fresno Bee*, December 10, 1989, Special Report: Teen Pregnancy, p. G2.

8. Kristin Luker, *Dubious Conceptions: The Politics of Teenage Pregnancy* (Cambridge, Mass.: Harvard University Press, 1996), p. 144.

9. Ibid., p. 184.

10. Dr. Claire Brindis, in Harriet Chiang, "Why Children Have Children," *San Francisco Chronicle*, March 8, 1998, Sunday Section, p. 4.

11. Alan Guttmacher Institute, *Facts in Brief: Teen Sex and Pregnancy*, September 1999, <http://www.agi-usa.org/pubs/fb_teen_sex.html> January 13, 2000.

12. Maynard, p. 36.

13. Ibid., p. 38.

14. U.S. Department of Health and Human Services, Public Health Service, Office of Population Affairs, Family Life Information Exchange, *Your Contraceptive Choices for Now, for Later* (pamphlet), n.d.

15. Luker, p. 144.

16. Alan Guttmacher Institute, *Facts in Brief.*

Chapter 4. Choices for Pregnant Teens

1. Elise Ackerman, "Who Gets Abortions and Why: Brenda Cummings," *U.S. News and World Report*, January 19, 1998, pp. 26–27.

2. Kristin Luker, *Dubious Conceptions: The Politics of Teenage Pregnancy* (Cambridge, Mass.: Harvard University Press, 1996), p. 155.

3. Alan Guttmacher Institute, *Facts in Brief: Teen Sex and Pregnancy*, September 1999, <http://www.agi-usa.org/ pubs/fb_teen_sex.html> January 13, 2000.

4. Alan Guttmacher Institute, *Sex and America's Teenagers* (New York: Alan Guttmacher Institute, 1994), p. 82.

5. Shai Linn, "The Relationship Between Induced Abortion and Outcome of Subsequent Pregnancies," *American Journal of Obstetrics and Gynecology*, May 1983, pp. 136–140.

6. J.R. Ashton, "The Psychosocial Outcome of Induced Abortion," *British Journal of Obstetrics and Gynecology*, December 1980, pp. 1115–1122.

7. Frederick H. Kanfer, Susan Englund, Claudia Lennhoff, and Jean Rhodes, *A Mentor Manual for Adults Who Work with Pregnant and Parenting Teens* (Washington, D.C.: Child Welfare League of America, 1995), pp. 67–81.

8. Ibid., p. 83.

9. Ibid., p. 85.

10. Ibid., pp. 75, 87–88.

11. Alan Guttmacher Institute, *Facts in Brief.*

12. C.A. Bachrach, "Adoption Plans, Adopted Children, and Adoptive Mothers," *Journal of Marriage and the Family*, vol. 48, 1986, p. 243.

13. Luker, p. 163.

14. Rebecca A. Maynard, ed., *Kids Having Kids: Economic Costs and Social Consequences of Teen Pregnancy* (Washington, D.C.: Urban Institute, 1997), p. 3.

15. David Popenoe, *Life Without Father* (New York: Martin Kessler, 1996), pp. 139–143.

16. F. Philip Rice, *The Adolescent: Development, Relationships, and Culture*, 11th ed. (Boston: Allyn and Bacon, 1992), pp. 448–449.

Chapter 5. The Consequences of Teen Pregnancy

1. Scott Trie, presentation at Teen and Parent Forum sponsored by Valley Children's Hospital, Fresno, Calif., September 12, 1998.

2. Sara McLanahan and Gary Sandefur, *Growing Up with a Single Parent: What Hurts, What Helps* (Cambridge, Mass.: Harvard University, 1994), p. 97.

3. Kristin Luker, *Dubious Conceptions: The Politics of Teenage Pregnancy* (Cambridge, Mass.: Harvard University Press, 1996), p. 108.

4. Rebecca A. Maynard, ed., *Kids Having Kids: Economic Costs and Social Consequences of Teen Pregnancy* (Washington, D.C.: Urban Institute, 1997), p. 302.

5. California State Board of Education, *Policy on Adolescent Pregnancy and Parenting* (paper), July 9, 1993 (national statistic).

6. *Kids' Count Missouri*, June 9, 1995, <http://oseda. missouri.edu/kidcat/reports/teenpreg/econcst.html> January 17, 2000.

7. Maynard, pp. 3–4.

8. Alan Guttmacher Institute, *Facts in Brief: Teen Sex and Pregnancy*, September 1999, <http://www.agi-usa.org/pubs/ fb_teen_sex.html> January 13, 2000.

9. Maynard, p. 71.

10. *Kids Count Data Book 1998* (Baltimore: Annie E. Casey Foundation, 1998), p. 7.

11. Alan Guttmacher Institute, *Sex Education and AIDS Education in the Schools: A Survey of State Policies, Curricula, and Program Activities* (New York: Alan Guttmacher Institute, 1989).

12. Maynard, pp. 184, 198.

13. Frank Furstenberg, Jr., J.A. Levine, and J. Brooks-Gunn, "The Children of Teenage Mothers: Patterns of Early Childbearing in Two Generations," *Family Planning Perspectives*, 22, no. 2, March–April 1990, pp. 54–61.

14. Maynard, p. 210.

15. *Campaign for Our Children,* n.d., <http://www.cfoc.org/statscost.html> January 17, 2000.

16. Maynard, p. 235.

17. Frank Furstenberg, Jr., J. Brooks-Gunn, and S. Philip Morgan, *Adolescent Mothers in Later Life* (Cambridge, Mass.: Cambridge University Press, 1987), p. 99.

18. Maynard, p. 308.

Chapter 6. Changing the Trends

1. Personal interviews, 1995–1998.

2. Bryan Strong and Christine DeVault, *The Marriage and Family Experience*, 6th ed. (Minneapolis: West, 1995), p. 334.

3. F. Philip Rice, *The Adolescent: Development, Relationships, and Culture*, 11th ed. (Boston: Allyn and Bacon, 1992), pp. 371–372.

Bode, Janet. *Kids Still Having Kids: People Talk About Teen Pregnancy*. New York: Franklin Watts, 1999.

Edelson, Paula. *Straight Talk About Teenage Pregnancy*. New York: Facts on File, 1998.

Hughes, Tracy. *Everything You Need to Know About Pregnancy*. New York: Rosen Publishing Group, 1997.

Jamiolkowski, Raymond. *A Baby Doesn't Make the Man: Alternative Sources of Power & Manhood for Young Men*. New York: Rosen Publishing Group, 1997.

Miller, Barbara. *Teenage Pregnancy & Poverty: The Economic Realities*. New York: Rosen Publishing Group, 1997.

Park, Jane, and Kathryn Muller. *Just the Facts: What Science Has Found Out About Teenage Sexuality & Pregnancy in the U.S.* Los Altos, Calif.: Sociometrics Corporation, 1998.

Simpson, Carolyn. *Coping with Teenage Motherhood*. New York: Rosen Publishing Group, 1997.

Stewart, Gail B. *Teen Fathers*. San Diego: Lucent Books, 1997.

Trapani, Margi. *Teenage Mothers Speak Out*. New York: Rosen Publishing Group, 1997.

Further Reading